T0380800

ALSO BY SUNDAY A POPOOLA

- Male and Female (Created He them)
- Images (Living behind the shadows)
- Living without stress
- The Bloody-Bloody gospel
- A people of power (God's big show)
- The Creative word
- The Anointing
- Be fruitful and multiply
- Goodwill unto men
- Victory over your adversary
- Three steps in Supernatural living
- Turning your scars to stars
- Born to reign
- How to receive healing

THE THIRD DIMENSION

SUNDAY A POPOOLA

WESTBOW
PRESS®
A DIVISION OF THOMAS NELSON
& ZONDERVAN

WestBow Press books may be ordered through booksellers or by contacting:

WestBow Press
A Division of Thomas Nelson & Zondervan
1663 Liberty Drive
Bloomington, IN 47403
www.westbowpress.com
844-714-3454

Unless otherwise indicated, scripture quotations are taken from the New King James Version. Copyright © 1982 by Thomas Nelson, Inc. Used by permission. All rights reserved.

Scripture quotations marked AMP are taken from the Amplified® Bible, Copyright © 1954, 1958, 1962, 1964, 1965, 1987 by The Lockman Foundation. Used by permission.

ISBN: 978-1-6642-8860-7 (sc)
ISBN: 978-1-6642-8859-1 (e)

Print information available on the last page.

WestBow Press rev. date: 01/05/2023

DEDICATION

I dedicate this book to Omowunmi Popoola, my companion in destiny; and to the new generation of the champions of faith who are crying out for more that is available, accessible, and obtainable in God; who are pressing into the higher calling of the Governor among the nations; who refuse to be satisfied with the mundane and temporal; who strongly crave, yearn, and aspire to see His kingdom come and His will done across the earth.

I pray this book will spark an enduring fire in you.

CONTENTS

PREFACE

A man's perception on issues determines his dimension in life. No man can operate beyond the level of his revelation. The truth is that the level of your revelation determines your stratum and height in life.

There is a sphere in which a man can live life at its best, a level that is supernatural and a realm where his full potential is realized. There is a dimension in God where the flawlessness of God's work in man is reached. That is what this book is all about.

Man was created in the image and likeness of God. He was meant to bear the nature of God and operate like Him on earth. He was made as God's regent to administer the earth on His behalf:

"Then God blessed them, and God said to them, 'Be fruitful and multiply; fill the earth and subdue it; have dominion over the fish of the sea, over the birds of the air, and over every living thing that moves on the earth'" (Genesis 1:28).

Man was given the mandate to have dominion over the earth. The word translated "dominion" is from the Hebrew root word mamlakah, which means "sovereign rule, kingdom, reign, or royal power." Adam walked in this realm and had the earth in total subjection until sin crossed his threshold through Satan's deception. He violated God's instruction not to eat of the tree of knowledge of good and evil. Influenced by his wife, he went on to eat the fruit and consequently lost the authority to rule the earth.

Man thus became depraved and subdued under the forces he was meant to rule over. Death, sickness, suffering, poverty, affliction, disasters, wars, wickedness, and the like became the outcome of man's rebellion against God. As the rebellion or rejection of God increased on earth, man's troubles also abounded.

World leaders and world bodies like the United Nations are working relentlessly to bring solutions to global problems. These efforts usually end in disappointment and failure. Until man rediscovers his roots in God and is properly connected to Him and His purpose, he is condemned to failure and malfunction.

After the fall of man, God committed Himself to man's redemption through the seed that was to come from the woman. In the fullness of time, Jesus Christ came in man's image through the woman and laid down His life, thus paying the full penalty for man's sin. He redeemed man and restored him to his original state. However, man's redemption cannot be said to be complete until he begins to function once more in the same realm of life in which Adam lived and operated before he sinned and fell.

Jesus came in the form of man and literally walked in that realm of dominion, signifying that the door is open again for us to enter in and walk in the same dominion. As the first man to walk in that realm after the fall of Adam, Jesus has presented this dimension and facet of life to all who come to God through Him. This is the realm of life where we can enjoy fullness, completeness, and total dominion through Jesus Christ.

While the delivery of redemption by God was made once and for all through Christ's death on the cross, the attainment of it by man takes a process. Presently, we have yet to see man walk in the realm of life and dominion in which both the first Adam and the last Adam (Jesus) walked.

Many who profess to be genuinely redeemed definitely have made great advancements in the transformation of their lives, but none of us can truly claim to be living in the realm of life that the first Adam lived in before the fall and, ultimately, the measure of life that Jesus lived. We are, therefore, yet to enter into full redemption heritage. What we have now is the "earnest" of our inheritance, or "down payment"; the fullness is to be possessed in this new day.

God is a God of plans; His purposes are progressive in nature. The Bible says, "He has made everything beautiful in its time." (Ecclesiastes 3:11) Understanding the times and seasons of God is very crucial in our walk with God and in acquiring our redemption rights. When we have insight into God's times and seasons, we can live more purposefully and effectively.

The world's greatest disaster and misfortune is the multitude of people who live without purpose or live for the wrong purpose. They deplete the earth instead of replenishing it as God commands. Many precious lives and resources are wasted because of ignorance of God's purposes, times, and seasons. Jesus indicted Israel for this:

He answered and said to them, "When it is evening you say, 'It will be fair weather, for the sky is red'; and in the morning, 'It will be foul weather today, for the sky is red and threatening.' Hypocrites! You know how to discern the face of the sky, but you cannot discern the signs of the times. (Matthew 16:2-3)

Where are we in God's calendar for the church universal, and what is God doing in the world presently? What lies ahead? Is there any hope for this world? These and more questions I will try to answer through biblical insight, prophecy, and contemporary events.

Discovery brings recovery. I believe you will receive the truth that will help you recover your purpose and destiny and enable you to contribute to the Creator's purpose in this world. It is my hope and prayer that this book will help you to understand what God is doing today and where you fit in. It is my desire that you are able to live purposefully and be on the cutting edge of what God is doing in this season by His Spirit.

May this world rejoice that you passed through it. May heaven celebrate your pilgrimage to this planet.

Sunday A Popoola (2011)

ACKNOWLEDGMENTS

My profound gratitude goes to my wife, who for years passionately cried out that more people needed to hear what God had given me to share with this generation. Your prayer and efforts to get this done are now coming to fruition. You are a tower of strength and blessing to me.

To all my admirers and contemporaries who have listened to me teach some of these materials in conferences and have encouraged me to publish some of them in book form.

To my son and daughter in the ministry, Tunde and Doyin Ewedemi, and their committee, who labored and invested their God-given resources to fashion a platform for my conferences where these messages were shared in the United Kingdom. You are really wonderful.

To David Arishemola, who suddenly appeared in my office one blessed day, asking to help transcribe my messages into books. Without your efforts, my desire to write this book would not have seen the light of day because of my busy schedule. Thank you for your unremitting efforts and hard work that gave birth to the first edition of this book.

To all members and friends of Word Communication Ministries and Christ Family Assembly Churches, who pray and support me in this great ministry. I am very grateful. You are a great people.

To all those who are too numerous to point out, whose books, messages, and friendship have inspired me and my work. Thank you. This is our book.

CHAPTER *1*

LIFE IS ESSENCE

Essence is what makes a person. When a man's essence is destroyed, he becomes a mere shadow of himself. A person devoid of his essence (a lunatic, for instance) is worse than a nonexistent thing; he is a liability and not an added value.

The English Dictionary defines essence as "the quality that makes something what it is." It is the most indispensable and central quality of anything. Your contribution to life is determined by your essence. The degree to which you can harness your essence, therefore, is the degree to which you can make a positive impact on the earth. Your essence makes sense out of your life. Essence harnessed is purpose exhibited.

Every man's purpose is predetermined by God: "Before I formed you in the womb I knew you; before you were born I sanctified you; I ordained you a prophet to the nations." Jeremiah 1:5. A man does not choose his purpose—he discovers it.

The word ordain is from the Hebrew root word nathan, which means "to bestow, to commit, to empower." Your essence empowers you for purpose. When purpose is not realized, essence is wasted. When essence is not harnessed, purpose is defeated. Your greatest discovery, therefore, is the discovery of your purpose, while your greatest recovery is the recovery of your essence. The Creator is the source of both.

God determines purpose and gives essence. True knowledge of God leads to discovery of purpose and recovery of essence. Your greatest pursuit, therefore, should be the pursuit of God: "But without faith it is impossible to please Him, For he who comes to God must believe that He is, and that He is a rewarder of those who diligently seek Him" (Hebrews 11:6). Also, " And you will seek Me and find Me, when you search for Me with all your heart" (Jeremiah 29:13).

A man's essence is actually the measure of the life of God that he is able to receive. We share God's essence, and the degree to which we as individuals are in harmony with God in any area of our lives is the degree to which we can exhibit our true essence in that area, fulfill our destiny, and achieve tremendous feats:"

Therefore, since we are the offspring of God, we ought not to think that the Divine Nature is like gold or silver or stone, something shaped by art and man's devising." Acts 17:29). Fulfilment of purpose is the essence of life. This comes through our connection to God.

We are already at the closing scene of world history, and God is rounding off the age. We therefore do not have time to play games when it comes to the issue of purpose. We want to redeem the time, be the best we can be, and maximize our lives for God's glory and the blessing of humanity.

It is equally imperative to understand and align our purpose with what God's priority is now and know what His strategy is to bring about that priority. Understanding and committing to God's purpose, timing, and strategy will deliver us from wasting our time, treasure, energy, and essence. It will empower us to make worthwhile and profitable decisions, be effective in our assignments, boost our impact, and make our lives uncomplicated and very productive. If we have the mind-set that maximizing profit and impact for the kingdom of God and making it to a heavenly reward are core, these would be the priorities of our lives now.

CHAPTER 2

THE THIRD DAY

We are living in a very crucial time, both in the history of the church of God and the entire human race. Economic meltdowns, wars, terrorism, human trafficking, disasters, the rising tide of rejection of oppressive governments, and dictatorship are all indices of these times.

For the church globally and also for the believer personally, it is of utmost importance to understand God's agenda and His strategy for accomplishment. This will put us at the cutting edge of what God is doing at this time across planet earth. My utmost aim in this chapter is to examine God's schedule for His church and determine her present position and standpoint in the Divine date book.

The people of the tribe of Issachar were known to be industrious agriculturists. They were also mentioned with honor for their heroic, laudable, and wise patriotism. They provided direction for the nation of Israel: "of the sons of Issachar who had understanding of the times, to know what Israel ought to do, their chiefs were two hundred; and all their brethren were at their command; "(1 Chronicles 12:32). The men of Issachar provided direction for the nation of Israel because they were able to discern the times and seasons. Whenever direction is lacking, confusion and destruction become inevitable. Any nation that lacks credible leaders is doomed. Leadership requires direction and discernment of the timing and seasons associated with it, as well as the will to take necessary actions.

At a certain time in the history of the Israelites, they were indicted because they failed to discern the timing and seasons of God's works and operations among them: "He answered and said to them, "When it is evening you say, 'It will be fair weather, for the sky is red'; and in the morning, 'It will be foul weather today, for the sky is red and threatening.' Hypocrites! You know how to discern the face of the sky, but you cannot discern the signs of the times."

(Matthew 16:2-3). They were off course as a nation because they could discern only natural things. Spiritually, they were undiscerning. The purposes of God require spiritual discernment. For the church to effectively and positively impact the world in this dispensation, she must understand the timing and seasons of God as well as God's intent and purpose for the world at this time.

There are three days in the calendar of God for His church. This is indicated in the book of Hosea chapter 6:1-2, "Come, and let us return to the Lord; for He has torn, but He will heal us; He has stricken, but He will bind us up. After two days He will revive us; on the third day, he will raise us up, that we may live in His sight"

The church is revived on the second day and raised up on the third day! The church of God today has experienced the first two days and is now making inroads into the third day. God operates outside the box of man's timing. The timing of man (chronos time) is based on seconds, minutes, hours, days, weeks, and years. God's pattern of time is called kairos, and He does not count time by the clock. Twenty-four hours make up a day in man's timing, while a thousand years are like a day in God's system of timekeeping: "But, beloved, do not forget this one thing, that with the Lord one day is as a thousand years, and a thousand years as one day" (2 Peter 3:8).

Scripture reveals two types of churches: the church in the Old Testament and the New Testament church. I want us to look at the New Testament church, which is also the end-time church. The New Testament Church is our focus.

THE NEW TESTAMENT CHURCH

The church began with the coming of Jesus, the pattern-Son, who came to the earth in 4 BC. Between this time and now is just over two thousand years, which is equivalent to two days in God's calendar. We have entered the third day (the third millennium), and we can certainly say that we are in the early hours of the third day.

God promised revival in the second day; that is, the second millennium of Christ. In the second day, Martin Luther was raised to proclaim the truth of the new birth, while the Holy Spirit–baptism revival led by William J. Seymour commenced at Azusa in 1906. The second day was the day of revival for the New Testament church. Presently, many Christians are busy converging at various places to pray for revival. That's alright, but the Lord wants to take us beyond revival. This may be a shocker to many, we have surpassed the era of revival. What God has in-store for us at this moment is not another revival, but the experience of God's perfection. The church has encountered the revival in the second day, and it has been awesome. The Pentecostal and charismatic movements characterized the revival. All the signs and wonders currently being experienced among us are features of God's second day.

In the third day, God will take us beyond revival and into His resurrection and restoration. He will resurrect and restore us to live in His sight. The phrase "live in His sight" connotes the church coming of age and becoming fully grown and mature, becoming exactly what God intended her to be. It entails a restoration to the state of Adam before he fell. Glory to God! At the moment, the church has not fully conformed to the picture conceived in the heart of God for her. The set standard of God for the church universal is that she be made glorious and triumphant as Adam was prior to his fall and as Jesus demonstrated throughout His earthly life.

"The Spirit Himself bears witness with our spirit that we are the children of God, and if children, then heirs—heirs of God and joint heirs with Christ, if indeed we suffer with him, that we may be also be glorified together. For I consider that the sufferings of this present time are not worthy to be compared with the glory which shall be revealed in us. For the earnest expectation of the creation waits for the manifestation of the sons of God. For the creation was subjected to futility, not willingly but because of him who subjected it in hope; because the creation itself also will be delivered from the bondage of corruption into the glorious liberty of the children of God. For we know that the whole creation groans and labors with birth pangs together until now. Not only that, but we also who have the firstfruits of the Spirit, even we ourselves groan within ourselves, eagerly waiting for the adoption, the redemption of our body. (Romans 8:16–23). The phrase sons of God in this context signifies a church that has attained perfection and maturity.

There are two Greek words used for son in the New Testament; the first is the word 'Teknon' which means, to beget or to bear a child; this gives prominence to the fact of birth. The second word is 'Huios' which means, Son in a generic sense, it stresses the dignity and character of the relationship.

'Huios' primarily signifies the relation of offspring to parent and not simply the birth as indicated by teknon. 'Huios' denotes relationship of character to the parent. In the narrative of His human birth Jesus is never designated as teknon or Teknon Theou, a child of God, but always ho Huios- The Son or the Son of God. Only the mother called him teknon Lk2:48. as she viewed Him in His Humanity.

Jesus never presents Himself in His God-Man consciousness as teknon of man or of God . He was only Huios denoting relationship or conformity of character with the Father-God not giving the idea He was a mere child of God. The difference between believers as children (tekna) of God and as Sons (Huios) is brought out in Romans 8:16,19;

"The Spirit Himself bears witness with our spirit that we are children (tekna) of God (Romans 8:16),

"For the earnest expectation of the creation eagerly waits for the revealing of the sons (huios)of God." (Romans 8:19).

Tekna refers to those who were born of God and have just the basic relationship as born again children of God. Huios refers to those who show maturity acting as sons whose lifestyle shows they are legitimate offspring by their likeness to God's character irrespective of gender.

The expression "Son of God is used of Jesus as a manifestation of His relationship with the Father or the expression of His sinless conformity to the Father's character. The Lord Jesus is never called teknon Theou, child of God as believers are. In John 1:12 tekna is used of new believers.

It is the manifestation of the Huios Theou that creation is waiting for, not the tekna Theou. Our frustration as believers lies in the fact that we remain as tekna Theo and want to operate as Huios Theou.

When Jesus died on the cross He birthed a seed or son (teknon), that is meant to grow into His likeness, who when fully grown, would give God a people on the earth who like Jesus would walk hundred percent in the Spirit. A people in whom God would be well pleased (huios Theou).

At river Jordan, when Jesus had been baptized, He came up immediately from the water; and behold, the heavens were opened to Him, and He saw the Spirit of God descending like a dove and alighting upon Him. And suddenly a voice came from heaven, saying, "This is My beloved Son (Huios), in whom I am well pleased." (Matthew 3:16-17).

It is clear that in the purpose of God He has fore-ordained a people who would be conformed to the image of His son (Huios), and would come forth in His likeness thereby establishing His kingdom on earth. "For whom He foreknew, He also predestined to be conformed to the image of His Son, that He might be the firstborn among many brethren." (Romans 8:29).

Jesus is God's pattern for Sonship.

The earth is subject to vanity, because the church has not reached her full maturity and seems helpless in the face of the satanic orchestrations being perpetrated on the earth.

The world is yet to fully know the church as she was conceived in the heart of God. The entire world is waiting for the manifestation and appearance of the mature, grown up, and established sons of God as they stand in their full salvation heritage. God is bringing the church into the day of release that will result in the emancipation and release of the creatures on earth from satanic bondage.

THE NUMBER "THREE".

The number "three", has scriptural significance. It signifies perfection or completion: "On that very day, some Pharisees came saying to him, Get out and depart here, for Herod wants to kill you.' And He said to them, 'Go, tell that fox, "Behold, I cast out demons and perform cures today and tomorrow and the third day, I shall be perfected"(Luke 13:31–32).

When the Lord Jesus said He would be perfected on the third day, He was speaking allegorically. The Amplified Version of the Bible gives a clearer picture of what He was declaring to the global church:

And He said to them, Go and tell that fox [sly and crafty, skulking and cowardly], Behold, I drive out demons and perform healings today and tomorrow, and on the third day I finish (complete) My course. (Luke 13:32 | AMP). Jesus said His work will be brought to completion on the third day, which is the day of perfection and completion. When Jesus died for man's sin, He rose on the third day. His work on earth will also be brought to completion or perfection in this third day.

The hour has come for the church to mature into her full stature so that she might fill the earth with God's glory. The church consists of her individual members; therefore, the third day is the season that believers can mature into full stature, realize their full potentials in God, manifest His glory, and occupy their sphere of influence in a way that will amaze unbelievers.

"Arise, shine; for your light has come! And the glory of the Lord is risen upon you. For behold, the darkness shall cover the earth, and deep darkness the people; but the Lord will arise over you, and His glory shall be seen upon you. The Gentiles shall come to your light, and kings to the brightness of your rising. Lift up your eyes all around and see: They gather together, they come to you; your sons shall come from far and your daughters shall be nursed at your side" (Isaiah 60:1–4). The hour for the rising of the sons of God is now.

CHAPTER 3

THE DIMENSIONS OF GOD

God is one essence, who manifests Himself in three distinct personalities. These three personalities make up the Godhead, or Trinity: God the Father, the Son, and the Holy Spirit.

The moves and workings of God from the beginning of creation to the end can also be categorized into three dimensions: creation, redemption, and restoration of all things. The three persons of the Godhead are fully involved in each of these moves of God, but only one of them takes preeminence at a time.

CREATION

At the time of creation, the Father had preeminence. Creation was His idea. He initiated it: "And God said, 'Let us make man in Our image, according to Our likeness; let them have dominion over the fish of the sea, over the birds of the air, and over the cattle, over all the earth and over every creeping thing that creeps on the earth'" (Genesis 1:26). He had preeminence from the time of creation till the end of the old covenant.

REDEMPTION

Jesus, God the Son, had preeminence in the work of redemption. He was the one who laid down His life as the sacrificial Lamb to pay the full penalty for the sins of humanity so that man can be given eternal life and a standing before God as though he had never sinned. "In Him we have redemption through His blood, the forgiveness of sins, according to the riches of His grace." (Ephesians 1:7).

RESTORATION

The third and final move of God is the restoration of man and all things to their original state. The one who takes over at this stage is the Holy Spirit. He is the one in command in the restoration plan of God. The restoration of all things is scheduled for the third day, and it is the final move of God that will bring an end to the present world where Satan exerts dominion.

Every believer who wants to be relevant in the third day must get to know the person of the Holy Spirit, have fellowship with Him, obey Him, and be sensitive to Him. He is the commander of the third day, and any believer who is disobedient or insensitive to Him will miss out on the move of God in this dispensation. Anyone who is serious about being relevant in this dispensation cannot afford to be ignorant of, or ignore the Holy Spirit: "But when the Helper comes, whom I will send to you from the Father, the Spirit of truth, who proceeds from the Father, He will testify of Me" (John 15:26).

Jesus made it abundantly clear that if He did not depart, the Holy Spirit would not come. This implies that the exit of the Lord Jesus to heaven ushered in another dimension of the move of God. Jesus left for heaven after completing His own assignment so that the Holy Spirit could take the purpose of God further on earth.

There are consistent patterns in Scripture to buttress this truth. This three-dimensional pattern of God's move is clearly seen throughout Scripture in various ordinances, instructions, parables, and teachings. Let's briefly examine some of them.

I. THE TABERNACLE IN THE WILDERNESS

The tabernacle in the wilderness had three sections. The first section, the outer court, was where the bronze laver and bronze altar were placed. The people came freely to make their sacrifices for their sins throughout the year: They would lay their hands on the unblemished sacrificial animal (symbolically passing their sins onto it), and then it would be offered.

This way, they received remission for their sins, but this did not remove the sin nature. They still kept sinning every day.

Metaphorically, the church of God commenced here. It signifies the era when church people were merely religious, but not delivered from sinning continually. Even the priesthood was composed of a group of priests who really did not know God. They preached the gospel to the people, but they themselves did not understand the intricacies of the things they handled. Many would get drunk, commit immorality, and carry out all sorts of atrocities and still come to the pulpit to preach the gospel.

We are faced with many such preachers and Christians of the outer court today: people who lack the revelation and the power of God in their lives. They have a form of religion but lack the power there of. These are men who live continually in immorality while also engaged in the ministry.

Next to the outer court was the second segment, which was called the Holy Place, or the tabernacle proper: "For a tabernacle was prepared: the first part in which was the lampstand, the table, and the showbread, which is called the sanctuary" (Hebrews 9:2). This sacred place was not meant for everybody. It had in it the golden lampstand, the incense altar, and the table of showbread. Only the consecrated priests were allowed there. They ministered and offered sacrifices based on the ordinances God had given.

The Holy Place in church history connotes the Pentecost experience in the church. The Pentecost experience involves being Spirit-filled, Spirit-instructed, Spirit-led, and Spirit-empowered. This is where believers are enabled to live holy lives, cast out devils, heal the sick, raise the dead, and perform signs and wonders. Those who have tasted of this experience can testify that it is wonderful. The Pentecost experience of the Holy Place was so awesome that many concluded that it was the last move of God in the church. On the contrary, there is still more in God. In the Holy Place, we still find the taint of sin and some lawlessness. This place, therefore, cannot contain God's presence, because He is utterly holy.

The tabernacle in the wilderness did not end at the Holy Place. There was one other place, called the Holy of Holies. And behind the second veil, the part of the tabernacle which is called the Holiest of All, which had the golden censer and the ark of the covenant overlaid on all sides with gold, in which were the golden pot that had the manna, Aaron's rod that budded, and the tablets of the covenant; and above it were the cherubim of glory overshadowing the mercy seat (Hebrews 9:3–5). This section contained the ark of the covenant, which was the symbol of God's presence. Only the high priest could enter this place, and that was once a year on Yom Kippur, The Day of Atonement.

He had to enter this place with extreme caution. He was dressed in his full priestly garment, which had bells attached to it, and then he had a long rope tied to his waist, with one end hanging outside the entrance of the Holy of Holies. As long as the bells tinkled, the people outside knew he was still alive. If he died inside and the tinkling of the bells was no longer heard, the rope tied on his waist would be used to drag his corpse out, since nobody else could enter the Holy of Holies except the high priest.

The third day is the era of ministering in the Holy of Holies. This is a new dawn in the move of God. All the things allowed in the era of the first two places of the tabernacle in the wilderness will be forbidden in this place. It will not be business as usual in this dispensation of the third day. It is an era of total holiness in the presence of God. In the third day dispensation, the Lord will raise a body of people who will go beyond the veil, enter His awesome presence. and manifest the glory of God on the earth. At the point of death of Jesus on the cross, the veil of the temple was thorn, Luke 23:44-45 says,

"Now it was about the sixth hour, and there was darkness over all the earth until the ninth hour. Then the sun was darkened, and the veil of the temple was torn in two".

In every dispensation, God always gives a foreshadow of what is to come. The Old Testament saints did not experience the fullness of what was about to unfold on the earth, but they had a foretaste so that they could be witnesses to us. "Therefore, we also, since we are surrounded by so great a cloud of witnesses, let us lay aside every weight and the sin which so easily ensnares us and let us run with endurance the race that is set before us" (Hebrews 12:1). God gave us this cloud of witnesses so that when the third day begins to unfold and God's prophetic voices begin to sound the alarm, the doubts of men will be drowned and overruled.

Extraordinary, astonishing, and unusual things are going to happen in this third day. The Lord is about to unleash on the earth an army of people the world has never seen the likes of. This army of people will be known as the Mature Church. We are about to see a church that is triumphant in all ramifications of life.

Whenever the Lord is about to do a significant thing, He raises up prophets who will sound the alarm: "Blow the trumpet in Zion, and sound an alarm in My holy mountain! Let all the inhabitants of the land tremble. . . . A people come, great and strong" (Joel 2:1–2).

II. THE THREE FEASTS

Three feasts were instituted in Israel:

"Three times a year all your males shall appear before the Lord your God in the place which He chooses: at the Feast of Unleavened Bread [Passover], at the Feast of Weeks [Pentecost], and at the Feast of Tabernacles; and they shall not appear before the Lord empty-handed" (Deuteronomy 16:16).

These three feasts speak of three stages in our journey towards maturing into sonship. They are three life-changing experiences in God for us as children of God. The first is the Feast of the Passover. This can be likened to the salvation experience when we repent of our sins and by faith accept that when Jesus Christ laid down His life on the cross, He fully paid the penalty for our sins. This was God's love in demonstration. Jesus' lifeblood was shed, and the demand of God's justice over our sins was satisfied. Then He was raised from the dead. When we come to Him in faith, our sins are forgiven and we are reconciled to God, thus becoming children of God (teknon).

The second feast is the Feast of Pentecost. This is synonymous to our experience of being baptized in the Holy Ghost. It is the point when we are endued with divine power to live victoriously, cast out devils, heal the sick, and preach the gospel effectively. This is when we begin to experience manifestation of signs and wonders as we exercise the authority of the Lord Jesus.

There is also a third feast called the Feast of Tabernacles (also known as the Feast of Ingathering). It is the place when we begin to experience the fullness of God, total conquest or total dominion. Many awesome things are made manifest for us in this feast.

III. THE THREE SONS OF NOAH

Noah's three sons (Shem, Japheth, and Ham) repopulated the world after it was destroyed by flood. The various moves of God from the era of Noah till this moment were championed by the descendants of these three sons one after the other.

The Lord was initially revealed to Israel, the descendants of Shem. They were the first champions of the move of God, and God's knowledge was made manifest to the entire world through them. God's covenant with Israel is still so strong today that even if the entire world rages against them, it cannot prevail. It is fatal to contend against Israel, because they were chosen by God to manifest His almightiness, love, glory, and power, and to woo the entire world to Him. God is not a racist, but His moves are progressive. From Israel, the knowledge of God went out to the sons of Japheth. These were the Europeans, Asians, and Americans whom God used to champion His next move. The Europeans took the gospel of Jesus Christ to Africa and other parts of the world and labored greatly, many of them losing their lives in the process.

The last move of God will be championed by the sons of Ham. These are Africans, the dark- complexioned people. This last move of God before the world will come to an end will be the most powerful ever seen on earth.

Each move of God builds on the previous. When Barack Obama became the president of the United States of America, God signaled to the world that we had entered the third day. Obama has a direct African descent, making the world's number one citizen a son of Ham. It is time for Africa to rise and shine and lead the world in God's purposes and plans. Africa is about to show forth the praises of God in a way the world has never seen or expected.

IV. NOAH'S ARK

Noah's ark had three levels, and the occupants of each level were different, also indicating three levels of existence.

Located at the first level was the ground floor, which served as the compartment for food. This indicates those who live to eat and whose life pursuit is survival. This is life at the basest level, and it is the world's greatest disaster because the world's greater population lives at this level, where a person lives without divine purpose. Ministries that are set up as a means of enriching the founders belong to this level. Though God may still use them one way or another, the real motive behind their setup is survival. This level depicts people who see ministry as a means of livelihood rather than as a means to ennoble humanity for God's glory.

It makes the heart shudder to observe that many people enter the ministry because of the high rate of unemployment ravaging the world. Ministry should be entered into with caution and on the basis of God's election and calling so that our work will not be works that will burn. "Each man's work will become manifest; for the Day will declare it, because it will be revealed by fire; and the fire will test each one's work, of what sort it is. If anyone's work which he has built on it endures, he will receive a reward. If anyone's work is burned, he will suffer loss; but he himself shall be saved, yet so as through fire" (1 Corinthians 3:13–15).

The second level was occupied by animals and birds. This level depicts those who live at the level of mere instinct (the fleshly and carnal level). At this level, many live for wrong purposes like fame, pleasure, or to oppress others. This is the picture of ministries that are self-driven. Such ministries pursue goals that are motivated by a desire to satisfy selfish drives and appetites. They are not driven by God, but by selfish ambitions. They pay lip service to glorifying the Lord with their existence and ministries, but they are really more concerned with what they will receive from God than what to give Him. They are so materialistic and worldly that their focus is more on the prestige rather than the responsibilities of the ministry. Many of the atrocities being committed today among ministers and believers is due to the fact that this is the level where the majority still dwell.

The third level was occupied by Noah and his family. Noah and the members of his family signify those who are made in the image of God. This level implies the purpose-driven life, a life lived entirely to fulfill God's plan and purpose. It is the life that pursues being conformed to the image of Christ, a life of impact and eternal consequence. Ministry at this level is God-focused and God-pursuing. Such ministries are not concerned with the mundane, and even though they will be blessed, they understand that things esteemed by men are inconsequential in the sight of God. The main focus of people at this level is to glorify God on the earth and walk in the true image of the Son of God. They walk in the commanding authority, character, and glory of Jesus Christ on earth.

People at this third level are those who are totally transformed into His image. The apostle Paul had this kind of pursuit. They are the ones who will conclude the great move of God in the midst of the earth.

Most of the things we have hitherto fancied, applauded, and called "success" are like filthy rags in the sight of God. They are mere elements of the second level.

V. THE LIFE OF JESUS

Jesus Christ, our perfect example and pattern, passed through three phases while on earth.

At His birth, He was called Jesus (Savior), one who would save His people from their sins: "And she will bring forth a son, and you shall call his name Jesus, for he shall save his people from their sins" (Matthew 1:21).

The second phase of Jesus' life was when He was anointed to fulfill His public ministry. After His baptism at the Jordan River by John the Baptist, the Holy Spirit came upon Him, and He became the Christ, the Anointed One: "Then Jesus, when He had been baptized, came up immediately from the water; and behold, the heavens were opened to Him, and He saw the Spirit of God descending like a dove and alighting upon Him" (Matthew 3:16). Also, we read, "How God anointed Jesus of Nazareth with the Holy Spirit and with power, who went about doing good, and healing all who were oppressed of the devil, for God was with him"(Acts 10:38).

The third level of Jesus' life occurred when He resurrected from the dead and became Jesus Christ, the Lord. All authority was given to Him in heaven and on earth. He got back what Adam had lost in Eden, and earth's dominion became His. He became the sovereign ruler over the earth and holds the title deed to this earth. Praise His holy name!

VI. THREE LEVELS OF THE GOSPEL

The first level is the gospel of Jesus, the Savior. This is the gospel of the new birth, the truth that Martin Luther had a revelation of and preached after the dead age of the church. The ministry of Martin Luther revolved around proclaiming the new birth; that is, salvation by faith.

The second level is the gospel of Jesus, the Christ. This entails baptism in the Holy Spirit, the anointing and manifestation of God's power. This was seen at the Azusa Street revival when the Lord visited William Seymour and filled him with the Holy Spirit. Based on this, the church came to the realization that the gospel of Jesus went beyond just preaching of His salvation. They understood that there was a need to get baptized in the Holy Spirit and demonstrate His power after the new birth.

Every new move of God is always resisted by the recipients of the former. When the baptism in the Holy Spirit hit the church on Azusa Street, it was resisted by many for years. In my country, Nigeria, when the baptism in the Holy Spirit came, those who received it were persecuted, called all kinds of derogatory names, and sent out of the then-established denominational churches. This led to the establishment of the Pentecostal churches, which has become a phenomenon in the country today. These Pentecostal (mostly independent) churches have been instrumental in fanning the revival in Africa to the big flame it is today.

The truth about the Holy Spirit baptism and the demonstration of signs and wonders, which was believed to be a delusion even though made clear in the Scriptures, is now accepted by many. This level of the gospel is about faith, healing, deliverance, miracles, prosperity, and signs and wonders.

The third level of the gospel is called the gospel of Jesus Christ, the Lord. This level of the gospel emphasizes the lordship of Jesus Christ, with Him reigning over all on the face of the earth. This level is the last emphasis that will be added to the first two levels of the gospel. This level entails subjugating all the powers and kingdoms of this world to the lordship of the Lord Jesus. This level speaks the message of dominion: everything must conform to the expressed will and pleasure of the Lord Jesus. Men will abandon their desires and plans to embrace His will for them.

Most of the things done at the moment in the church are about us and not Him. The present-day church has been taught to see God as a means to man's end, using Him to achieve our selfish ambitions and varied purposes. But God is not a means to anybody's end—He is the end of all things!

You know Jesus' lordship when you surrender all things unto Him, allowing Him to have preeminence in every facet of your life. The lordship of Jesus is about doing everything His way and not your way. You cannot preach the gospel of the last days if you do not personally know the lordship of Jesus in your life. That means He dictates everything in your life.

I have pioneered nineteen viable churches in Africa, with another two in England. Presently, a five-thousand-seat auditorium is near completion at my base in Nigeria. Suddenly the Lord told me that I was done with pastoring. This meant He expected me to take my eyes away from these churches and face the next assignment He had for me. Since I am acquainted with His lordship, I left all this to concentrate on His next plan for me.

Anyone who had not come to terms with the lordship of Jesus would have found it difficult to let go of those churches. Such a person would not want to let go of his comfort zone. It takes knowing the lordship of Jesus to let go of your comfort zone and face the next phase of your life and ministry. It is like leaving certainty to pursue uncertainty. You need to understand that the uncertainty of God is more real than all the certainties of this world put together.

When you are acquainted with the lordship of Jesus, you cannot dictate your next destination. You are bound to follow only God's plans, allowing them to overrule your own plans. Even after surrounding yourself with everything you love, when the Lord tells you to move, you must move. This is nonnegotiable.

It is falsity that every pastor must build a megachurch. The fact that a man pastors a megachurch does not mean he is more successful than others who do not. This is because the callings of God on men are different. It is worldly to measure your success based on your acquisitions. God's assessment differs from men's assessment. Your faithfulness in doing precisely what God asked you to do is the yardstick for measuring success.

According to God, a man's success is measured by his adherence to God's plan for him. The lordship of Jesus Christ cannot be perfected in the life of a man who assesses himself by the standards of the world. Sadly, many people are delving into competition because they are measuring themselves by such standards.

However, this is not an excuse to be contented with smallness and stagnancy in your endeavors. There is a vast difference between accepting the plans of God for you and accepting the stagnancy imposed by ignorance and the devil. God expects you to make His plan for you successful. He wants your coast enlarged, because He is a big God. Receive every grace and wisdom made available to you, diligently do what you are instructed to do and trust God and be grateful for the results He gives.

Although the Lord expects you to be fervent and faithful and fruitful, you need to remember that only He gives increase. Many people have been trapped by the devil into occult practices in an effort to grow their ministries quickly. Your job is to follow the trend of God's increase for you. Do not force the increase by yourself.

Noah preached for 120 years but had just seven members. By the world's standards, he might have been called a failure, but God pronounced him a success because he saved the world. Those seven people with him gave birth to the nearly seven billion living presently on the face of the earth.

An evangelist was miserable after organizing a big crusade, because the attendance was poor. Since he was acquainted with Jesus' lordship, he preached as if millions of people were attending the crusade. Unknown to him, there was a boy in a corner who listened to his sermon and gave his life to Jesus Christ. That boy who got saved became a renown evangelist that did mighty exploits for the Lord. The evangelist thought the crusade was a failure because it had been so poorly attended, but the product of the crusade turned out to be a great success. I believe the Lord instructed him to organize the crusade so that a bigger evangelist would receive the salvation of Jesus Christ.

Anyone can count the number of seeds in an orange fruit, but only God knows the number of fruits that will come from each seed. You cannot fully determine or measure the extent of God's plan for your life.

The Lord expects you to execute His plan with all your power and might, but you must make sure that you implement it unto the Lord and not unto men. Stop being a man pleaser. Rather, strive to please God in all you do.

Some months ago, I was scheduled to minister at an international conference beyond the shores of my beautiful country, Nigeria. One of the women who was to attend to certain things at the conference had just lost her first son, so we assumed that because she had just been bereaved, she would not show up at the conference. Surprisingly, she came. After the conference, she intimated with what had happened, that she had come because the Lord wanted her to be available. She said she would not allow the demise of her son to stop doing what God wanted for her life. This is a clear picture of someone who is acquainted with the lordship of Jesus. Although she was in pain, she surrendered to the lordship of Jesus Christ.

We have been called to preach the gospel of His lordship and dominion in this dispensation. Many people are busy preaching about dominion, while being naïve as to what it entails. The word dominion simply means enforcing the kingdom of God upon territories. It is not about procuring new vehicles and mansions or acquiring material largesse. I know many unbelievers who own those things, and if acquisition of affluence is dominion, then the people of the world have it. In reality, dominion is about bringing the kingdom of God to bear on all spheres of social impact.

VII. THE SOWER'S SEED

In the parable of the sower as told by Jesus, the seed that fell on good ground produced three types of harvest: thirtyfold, sixtyfold, and a hundredfold. I want to compare this with the various types of believers there are: thirtyfold, sixtyfold, and hundredfold believers.

Thirtyfold believers are carnal Christians. They are 30 percent spiritual and 70 percent carnal.

Sixtyfold Christians are committed Christians. This category portrays believers who are 60 percent spiritual and 40 percent carnal. Most Christians function at this level. One adage common among Christians at the moment is that nobody is perfect because we are all human. People in this category hide behind the canopy of this adage. However, before this world comes to an end, there will be human beings who will walk in the fullness of Christ. They will walk in the fullness of His power, character, and glory.

I know many people might conclude that this is impossible, but Scripture tells us that with God all things are possible. This feat will not be achieved by esoteric teaching broadcast all over the place. It will be attained by the outpouring of the Spirit of God: "And it shall come to pass afterward that I will pour out My Spirit on all flesh; your sons and your daughters shall prophesy, your old men shall dream dreams, your young men shall see visions" (Joel 2:28).

This prophecy by Joel has been misconstrued by many. The Scriptures do not only say that God will pour out His Spirit on all His people, but also on all the flesh of His people. When the Spirit of God is poured upon all the flesh of a person, every aspect of his flesh will surrender to the spirit and cease to function in carnality. Everything about him will begin to function in by Spirit of God.

The third level refers to those who fall into the category of a hundredfold. These people are a hundredfold spiritual. There is no speck of carnality in them: "Love has been perfected among us in this: that we may have boldness in the day of judgment; because as he is, so are we in this world" (1 John 4:17). This verse makes it clear that we will be like Him while we are still in this world, and those who accept this truth will be like Him before departing for heaven. However, many people are of the opinion that they will be like Him only when they get to heaven.

When the Lord Jesus was on the earth physically, the anointing upon Him was limitless: "For he whom God has sent speaks the words of God, for God does not give the Spirit by measure" (John 3:34). Nothing could withstand Him while He was physically on earth because the anointing of God upon Him was without measure. Everything in nature obeyed Him. He spoke to the storm, the fig tree, and even the dead, and they all obeyed. Jesus spoke to leprous skin, and it became as fresh as a baby's skin. In this dispensation, the Lord is raising up a company of people whose anointing will be limitless and who will operate in the full stature of Christ Jesus. "And He Himself gave some to be apostles, some prophets, some evangelists, some pastors and teachers for the equipping of the saints, for the work of the ministry, for the edifying of the body of Christ till we all come to the unity of the faith and of the knowledge of the Son of God, to a perfect man, to the measure of the stature of the fullness of Christ." (Ephesians 4:11–13). These verses show that the end result of their assignment is to ensure that the saints attain perfection unto "the stature of the fullness of Christ."

Man's unbelief cannot change the efficacy of the Word of God. Since God said this will be accomplished at His stipulated time, and since it is clear that there will be no apostle, prophet, evangelist, pastor, or teacher in heaven, then these verses of Scripture will be fulfilled here on earth.

Faith comes by hearing the Word of God, and it enables us to please God. When you believe what God says, His Spirit will come upon you to conform you to His Word. Irrespective of your present spiritual state, you can become a hundredfold Christian.

After our salvation, the Holy Spirit is given to us as the earnest of our possession. The scripture says, "in Him you also trusted, after you heard the word of truth, the gospel of your salvation; in whom also, having believed, you were sealed with the Holy Spirit of promise, who is the guarantee of our inheritance until the redemption of the purchased possession, to the praise of His glory. (Ephesians 1:13–14). The Greek word used to describe the word earnest in this context in the King James Version is "arrhabon" which means "pledge or down payment." The Holy Spirit is the guarantee, or pledge of our divine inheritance. He is the foretaste, the down payment, or the firstfruits of our heritage in anticipation of His full redemption and our acquiring complete possession of it to the praise of His glory.

Every charismatic move the church has so far experienced is just a down payment or foretaste, not the full payment. The real inheritance is about to unfold and manifest. What we have now is in anticipation of what is about to come. The firstfruits are not the end of the harvest, just as a down payment is not the full payment. The full payment (the limitless anointing that was on Jesus Christ) is coming. Everything on earth is subject to this anointing.

Even in the Old Testament, certain people were given a foretaste of this full inheritance. Elijah stood in the presence of King Ahab and declared the full counsel of God. He did not come out of some carnal activities to speak to Ahab, but rather, he spoke out of the presence of God: "And Elijah the Tishbite, of the inhabitants of Gilead, said to Ahab: "As the Lord God of Israel lives, before whom I stand, there shall not be dew nor rain these years except at my word." (1 Kings 17:1). Elijah was able to open or close the heavens because he stood and spoke by divine authority. A person is incapacitated from speaking by divine authority when he is subject to carnality. Backed by divine authority, Elijah's words brought King Ahab to his knees. Ahab was compelled to send emissaries to look for Elijah, but they could not find him. However, based on God's instructions, Elijah appeared before the king. He eventually rattled the king and his four hundred and fifty prophets of Baal on Mount Carmel. Elijah had command over King Ahab and his prophets because power had changed hands. This is where the third day church is going. She will judge all the kingdoms of this world and bring all the unrighteous rulers of the world to their knees.

The church of the third day is composed of hundredfold Christians who will declare the counsel of God strictly from the presence of God. They will dwell there permanently, with no iota, scrap, or speck of carnality in their operations. They will be caught up to the throne of God, though operating on earth.

Ephesians 2:6 says, "And raised us up together and made us sit together in heavenly places in Christ Jesus." The third day church will experience this verse of Scripture practically, not just theoretically. She will declare the expressed counsel of God from heavenly places in Christ. She will speak as if God Himself is speaking. This is because she will not speak from her own mind, but by the Spirit of God.

VIII. THREE CATEGORIES OF PEOPLE

Saint John wrote his epistle to three categories of Christians:

"I write to you, little children, because your sins are forgiven you for His name's sake; I write to you, fathers, because you have known Him who is from the beginning. I write to you, young men, because you have overcome the wicked one." (1 John 2:12–13).

The first class is the "little children." John wrote that their sins are forgiven. Forgiveness of sin entails salvation. All that spiritual little children are acquainted with is salvation. They are dependent and vulnerable, always needing to be helped.

The next is the category of "young men." Young men are full of strength and vigor, and they know the acts of God. They can be likened to the church of this generation, which is vast in demonstrating signs and wonders and is aggressive against satanic tendencies, knowing only the acts of God (how to prosper, heal the sick, and cast out devils).

There is a third generation that is greater than this present generation. This is the generation that knows Him, and these are the ones who are conformed to His image and know His will and will bring His works to completion. The hour has come for the church to stop seeking only His acts; it is time to seek Him. It is time to stop seeking to build human empires and start seeking His purpose on the face of the earth.

IX. THREE LEVELS OF PRIESTHOOD

The priesthood is on the verge of leaving church buildings. It will no longer be in the sanctuaries, but on what I call the "seven mountains of social impact"

At the Shemite stage of the church, the priesthood was in the sanctuary and focused on spirituality and ordinances.

At the Japhethite stage, the priesthood was interwoven with intellectuality. They coupled the gospel with projects like hospitals, schools, and other forms of intellectual development.

The Hamite stage is the last priesthood. It is the priesthood of servanthood, which will bring pragmatic actions and manifestations. At this stage, the priesthood will be appointed upon communities, regions, and territories. It will no longer be a priesthood over church buildings, as in the Shemite stage. It will be a priesthood that bring practical solution to personal, community and national needs and problems of humanity through spiritual inspiration and enabling.

Presently, the European continent is greatly threatened by invasion of Islam. Muslims do not organize crusades or television evangelism like the church, yet they are systematically taking over Europe. This happened because they have engaged the culture. They have quietly and strategically planted disciples of Islam everywhere in the culture. The devil stole the strategy God meant for the church and gave it to the Muslims and they are running with it with commitment.

There are three heavens. The first heaven is called the atmospheric heaven. It is the place where demons and other satanic spirits operate. The second heaven is the planetary heaven, where planets are situated. The third heaven is the place where God resides and where the apostle Paul was taken. The third day church will not operate from the first two heavens, but from the place where the throne of God is situated. She will operate at the level that demons cannot reach and will be seated with Christ above the atmospheric and planetary heavens.

The army of Gideon that had victory over the Midianites was a third-dimension army. This was how they were chosen by the Lord: "And the Lord said to Gideon,

"The people who are with you are too many for me to give the Midianites into their hands, lest Israel claim glory for itself against me, saying, 'My own hand has saved me'" (Judges 7:2). When Gideon called the people of Israel to battle with the Midianites, thirty-two thousand people responded. After they assembled, God looked at them and concluded that they were too many to fight His battle. He told Gideon to instruct those who were afraid to return home. Twenty-two thousand men returned home in a jiffy. The battle of the Lord cannot be fought by people who have fearful hearts. He needs people who have hearts of faith. Scripture tells us that only those with hearts of faith can please the Lord. Faithless people cannot fight His battle. When those with fearful hearts departed, there were ten thousand men left. The Lord insisted that the ten thousand men who remained were still too many to fight His battle, so He instructed Gideon to take them to the river to drink. A large percentage of those who drank from the river lapped the water with their tongues. They were so engrossed in the water they were drinking that they lost sight of the battle ahead of them. They behaved as if their lives depended on what they ate or drank. Those whose bellies are their god cannot fight the battle of the Lord. They are too comfortable with fighting the battles of their bellies. Only three hundred men bowed down upon their knees to drink from the river. They used their hands to take water to their mouths while they looked ahead; unlike those who buried their heads in the water lapping with their tongues. Though they drank from the river, they were vigilant and focused. They did not allow what they were drinking to deter their focus from the battle that lay ahead of them. They did not live to eat or drink, but to fight the Lord's battle.

The third day church is made up of a company of believers who eat and drink for the battle ahead of them and not vice versa. They are focused on what the Lord is about to do through them.

Many believers at the moment are battling for what they will eat and drink. They live for their daily bread instead of living for God. They are like those who lapped the water with their tongues, so engrossed with making a livelihood that they lose sight of what the Lord is doing. They live to eat and drink instead of eat and drink to live. Scripture, however, says we are gods. A person loses sight of being a god when he behaves like a dog.

The Lord concluded that only the three hundred who were vigilant and focused would fight the battle. They fought and won the battle because they did not fight by their might, but by His Spirit. The Lord is still in the business of fighting the battle of His children, but He fights only on behalf of those who are vigilant and focused on the mightiness of His Spirit.

Presently, many people are fighting various battles in their lives. These battles can be won only when they are vigilant and focused on what the Lord is doing. Battles are not fought and won by what we drink or eat. They are won by the might of His Spirit. We must be vigilant and focused on the Holy Spirit in order to subdue and win the battles in our lives.

The three hundred men who were chosen did not win the battle with sophisticated weapons. They won by the might of the Spirit of God. It does not matter what kind of weapon you possess to fight your battle; be assured that your battles will be won when you are focused on the might of His Spirit.

Scripture says, "For by strength no man will prevail" (1 Samuel 2:9). Battles are not won by human strength; they are fought and won by the strength of God. The might of His Spirit is not released to a person who relies on his own strength, since God will not give His glory to anyone.

THE THIRD DAY

Jesus completed the redemption work with His resurrection on the third day, and the church of God will live in the sight of God on the third day. If you are going to be on the cutting edge of what the Lord is doing, you have to be aware of His timing and patterns. You cannot afford to live your life or run your ministry as others before you have done. You need to shift with the proceedings of the third day.

Have you noticed that if you are writing a letter at 12:01 a.m., you might put the date of the previous day, even though it's another day? This is because you still have the mind-set that you are still in the previous day. In the same way, there are strong tendencies that, although we have crossed to the third day, make us think that we are still in the second day. We cannot afford to practice Christianity as it was done in the second day, because we have been ushered into the third day. We are in the third day and must do what the Lord expects of us in this day: to live as a third day believer. As time progresses, the day will dawn, and the Day Star will rise upon us.

CHAPTER 4
THE HUMAN DIMENSIONS

THE THREE SONS OF NOAH

As we have already noted, the present population of the world descended from the three sons of Noah: "These were the families of the sons of Noah, according to their generations, in their nations; and by these the nations were divided on the earth after the flood" (Genesis 10:32). These three sons constitute the various peoples and families living presently on the earth.

The oldest of the three sons, Shem, is known to be the forefather of the Shemites. The Shemites are the people residing in the Middle East. The responsibility of maintaining man's spiritual life was given to the sons of Shem.

Ham was the second son of Noah. The name Ham means "burnt, swarthy, and black." He is the forefather of the Hamitic Africans and was given the responsibility of rendering service to the earth. The responsibility of the sons of Ham is to guarantee the physical survival and dominion of man on the earth.

Japheth was the youngest son, and he is known to be the forefather of the present-day Europeans, who brought intellectuality and education to the earth. The sons of Japheth were responsible for the enlargement of human thoughts and the elaboration of the contributions of the sons of Shem and Ham.

The differences among these three sons do not make one superior to the other. These differences exist simply as a part of God's economy. The issue is not of worth, but the uniqueness of the contribution of each of them, both to themselves and to mankind as a whole. "God, who made the world and everything in it, since He is Lord of heaven and earth, does not dwell in temples made with hands. Nor is He worshiped with men's hands as though he needed anything, since He gives to all life, breath, and all things. And He has made from one blood every nation of men to dwell on all the face of the earth and has determined their preappointed times and the boundaries of their dwellings, so that they should seek the Lord, in the hope that they might grope for Him and find Him, though He is not far from each one of us; for in Him we live and move and have our being, as also some of your own poets have said, "For we are also His offspring." (Acts 17:24–28).

The lives of the three sons of Noah connote the three dimensions operational in the life of man. These human dimensions are in certain patterns that are observable.

—Human composition: Every human being is made up of a spirit, soul, and body. Man is a spirit, has a soul, and resides in a body.

- Human spirit: man's spirituality; the development of which was championed by the sons of Shem.
- Human soul: man's intellectuality; which development was championed by the sons of Japheth.
- Human body: man's physical ability for practical work this is being championed by the descendants of Ham.

—Human needs: The needs of every man are in three categories:

- Spiritual needs
- Intellectual needs
- Physical needs

The human world: Man lives in three worlds:

- The world of thoughts: Thoughts are contents of cognition. They connote the sons of Shem, who brought the knowledge of God to humanity.

- The world of feelings: Feelings entail emotional or moral sensitivity. This represents the sons of Japheth, who invaded the earth with education, science, and technology.
- The world of things: Things, in this context, connote achievements and feats; it entails results. Every man has the capability to attain results. A world of things represents the sons of Ham, who are on the verge of demonstrating the practical move of God on the earth.

Human capacities and activities: Every man has capacities that can be categorized into three basic groups:

- Worship: This implies the spiritual capability of a man.
- Philosophy: In this context, it connotes the intellectual and educational capabilities in man.
- Technology: This entails the practical application of human capabilities.

These dimensions need to be developed and cultivated equally for a man to have a complete personality. When one or two of them are underdeveloped or more developed than the others, there is an imbalance.

Skill and knowledge with no form of spirituality is absolutely dangerous. On the other hand, abnormality sets into the life of a person who concentrates only on worship and neglects technical competence or intellectual development. Overemphasis on a man's spiritual needs hinders his social development. In the same vein, overemphasis on intellectuality and physical needs limits man and can also be detrimental.

THREE DELEGATIONS OF PEOPLE WHO SOUGHT FOR JESUS

—The shepherds: The shepherds who sought Jesus Christ at His birth in Bethlehem were from the lineage of Shem.

—The wise men: The lineage of the wise men from the East who brought gifts to Jesus Christ at His birth was not specified. However, their identity can be deduced from the gifts they brought: gold, frankincense, and myrrh. These gifts must have come from Africa, possibly Ethiopia, southern Arabia, or Somalia. Sons of Ham. These areas were sources for trade suppliers going from southern Arabia to the Mediterranean.

Certain Greeks: "Now there were certain Greeks among them who came up to worship at the feast. Then they came to Philip who was from Bethsaida of Galilee and asked him, saying, "Sir, we wish to see Jesus." (John 12:20–21). These Greeks were from the genealogy of Japheth:

THE PREACHING OF THE GOSPEL

The gospel was preached after Jesus' resurrection to these three groups of people:

The Israelites:
"Men of Israel, hear these words: Jesus of Nazareth, a Man attested by God to you by miracles, wonders and signs which God did through Him in your midst, as you yourselves also know." (Acts 2:22). These men of Israel were from the lineage of Shem:

Cornelius the centurion:
"There was a certain man in Caesarea called Cornelius, a centurion of what was called the Italian Regiment, a devout man, one who feared God with all his household, who gave alms generously to the people and prayed to God always. . . . And they said, "Cornelius the centurion, a just man and one who fears God and has a good reputation among all the nation of the Jews, was divinely instructed by a holy angel to summon you to his house and to hear words from you." (Acts 10:1–2, 22). Cornelius was from the lineage of Japheth.

—The Ethiopian eunuch:
"So he arose and went. And behold, a man from Ethiopia, a eunuch of great authority under Candace the queen of the Ethiopians, who had charge of all her treasury, and had come to Jerusalem to worship, was returning. And sitting in his chariot, he was reading Isaiah the prophet. Then the Spirit said to Philip, "Go near and overtake this chariot." (Acts 8:27–29). The third branch of people who heard the gospel after the resurrection of the Lord Jesus was the Ethiopian eunuch. He was from the lineage of Ham:

THOSE WHO PLAYED OFFICIAL
ROLES AT THE CRUCIFIXION

The descendants of the three sons of Noah were involved officially at the crucifixion of the Lord Jesus.

Mutual responsibility: The Jews (the sons of Shem) were mutually responsible for His crucifixion. "And all the people answered and said, "His blood be on us and on our children." (Matthew 27:25).

Carrying the cross: "A man named Simon, a Cyrenian, was made to carry the cross for Jesus. The Cyrenian was a descendant of the sons of Ham. "Now as they led Him away, they laid hold of a certain man, Simon, a Cyrenian who was coming from the country, and on him they laid the cross that he might bear it after Jesus. (Luke 23:26).

The execution: The execution of the Lord Jesus was carried out by Roman soldiers. Romans are from the lineage of Japheth.

CHAPTER 5

THE THIRD DAY CHURCH

In this chapter, I want to outline some of the characteristics of the third day church.

As the army of the Lord, the church has been ordained by God to bring His purpose to perfect completion, so she will operate directly from His presence and put all His enemies under His feet. The third day church will battle for the Lord, not for selfish interests or ambitions. Her single focus will be to unlock the fullness of God's glory on the face of the earth. "The Lord said to my Lord, 'Sit at My right hand, till I make Your enemies Your footstool.' The Lord shall send the rod of your strength out of Zion. Rule in the midst of your enemies!" (Psalm 110:1–2). What David declared here is for the end times, and it will come to pass in this third day. Through Zion, the Lord will make the enemies of Jesus His footstool. The church will enforce the victory of Jesus over His enemies practically on earth; He is already seated at the right hand of the Father in heaven. The third day church will do it on His behalf.

The exceeding strength of the Lord Jesus will be made visible through us as we subdue the kingdoms of this world and its evil systems and put them under His feet. The third day church will take over the scene as the Lord places believers as priests over the seven mountains of culture: politics, commerce, education, science and technology, the arts, religion, and families.

The third day church will showcase the sons of God, and the earth will be filled with "saviors" who will demonstrate great power with incredible signs and wonders. They will hold sway over authorities, powers, territories, and nations. Sickness, disease, and death will not be able to conquer them.

There will be a reenactment of something that happened to the Israelites in the wilderness: there will be no feeble one in the third day church. In many of our crusades, we have seen the dead raised, the sick healed, the blind given sight, cripples walking, and the dumb speaking, yet there were many who did not receive their miracles. Presently, at crusades and healing meetings organized around the world, not everybody is privileged to receive their miracles. In this third day, however, everyone will receive their miracles.

"When evening had come, they brought to Him many who were demon-possessed. And He cast out the spirits with a word and healed all who were sick" (Matthew 8:16). When the Lord Jesus was on the earth physically, everyone received their healing at His crusades. The church of God is coming to that phase in the third day as the church reveals the love, power, and glory of God in its full intensity.

This following verse of Scripture is a prophecy that will be fulfilled: "For behold, the darkness shall cover the earth, and deep darkness the people; but the Lord will arise over you, and His glory will be seen upon you" (Isaiah 60:2). This prophecy was given, not just to excite us, but as something to be experienced. Presently, however, the church appears to be helpless in the face of darkness parading itself in the nations. The best she can do is to condemn governments, but nowhere in the Scriptures are we told that the governments across the earth will proffer solutions to the darkness flourishing in their nations. The church of God is the solution to the problems ravaging the nations, not the governments. "For unto us a Child is born, unto us a Son is given; and the government shall be upon His shoulder and His name will be called Wonderful, Counselor, Mighty God, Everlasting Father, Prince of Peace" (Isaiah 9:6). The government of the entire earth is on the shoulder of the Lord Jesus. The shoulder of a person is not found on his head, but on his body. The church of God is the body of Christ, and she will rule the earth with a rod of iron. "Your people shall be volunteers in the day of your power; in the beauties of holiness, from the womb of morning, you have the dew of your youth" (Psalm 110:3). The King James Version of the first part of this scripture says, "Thy people shall be willing in the day of thy power." When God's power is revealed, His church will be willing. The word willing in this context connotes that the church will have the faith to embrace the fullness of her redemption. No longer will the world need to question God's ability or His power to save, heal, or deliver. It will be obvious.

Since God is not limited by time, space, or anything else, the third day church will not be limited. She will translate the kingdom of this world into the kingdom of God and His Christ. She will usher in the King of Kings in the fullness of His glory—not in weakness, but in great triumph. The third day church is a triumphant church. She is the church that will be raptured and returned in the millennium. She is the glorious church that will reign with Christ in the new era.

"Arise, shine; for your light has come! And the glory of the Lord is risen upon you" (Isaiah 60:1). This is not the time to try to figure out how these things will come into manifestation. God will do whatever He promises to do, and He cannot relent on His word. What you need to do is to arise in your heart and have the faith to embrace the truth of God. You are alive and privileged to be a part of what the Lord will be doing in the third day church. The singular fact that you are reading this book shows that the hand of God is on you and that He has chosen you to demonstrate His power at this hour.

This is the most passionate hour in the history of the church, and you should be glad to witness and experience the emergence of the glorious church. It does not matter what you are going through at the moment; what matters is where the Lord is taking you. You might be going through difficult times, but God's unlimited power and glory are about to break forth in your life. Rejoice! Your redemption is now.

CHAPTER **6**

THE EARTH IS THE LORD'S

Does the devil have the right to exercise dominion on earth? This question has given rise to heated debates even among believers, and as is usually the case when an issue is not properly addressed, it has resulted in confusion and disturbance.

The devil takes advantage of anyone who is ignorant of his devices, but when a man comes to the realization of a truth, he is delivered from all sorts of skepticism and endless fables: "Lest Satan should take an advantage of us; for we are not ignorant of his devices" (2 Corinthians 2:11).

Many people, including believers, believe that the devil is meant to have a hold on the earth. They believe that the Lord Jesus will come and take His people out of the earth while the devil continues to have preeminence. This explains why most believers do nothing meaningful for the Lord while living on earth. They are in a hurry to go to heaven so they can escape the so-called dominion of the devil on the earth.

First and foremost, you need to understand that the devil did not create the earth, so it does not belong to him. It is not his legitimate heritage. No one can have perpetual preeminence over what does not rightfully belong to him except in a situation where the rightful owner remains in ignorance about his rights.

God created the earth for His purpose, and this does not include ceding or relinquishing the earth to the devil. If the devil had absolute preeminence over planet earth, it would signify that he had conquered the Lord, which is not possible. God is not going to allow the devil to have continual dominion on earth.

The Lord gave the earth to man as his inheritance, his home and made him the legitimate ruler. God also gave him absolute authority over the earth: "The heaven, even the heavens are the Lord's, but the earth He has given to the children of men" (Psalm 115:16). As far as God is concerned, man is supposed to have full control over the earth. When Adam obeyed the voice of Satan and disobeyed God, he submitted authority to Satan. Romans 6:16 says "Do you not know that to whom you present yourselves slaves to obey, you are that one's slaves whom you obey, whether of sin leading to death, or of obedience leading to righteousness?" Adam turned his legal dominion over into the hands of God's enemy, Satan. In redemption, God in Christ fully paid the penalty of man's sin, destroyed spiritual death in man, eradicated the nature of the devil in man's nature, and set man free from satanic authority, restore to man eternal life which is the nature of God and the authority lost to Satan. All who accept the redemption God give through Jesus are restored to sonship with God and dominion over Satan and his works. God joined with man in the incarnate Christ to deal with Satan's legal hold on man and take back man's rightful inheritance to give back to man.

In these days in which the devil is raising evil protégés to fill the various mountains of culture, the Lord is going to match their evil orchestrations with sons of God who will rise in power of the Spirit and bring every evil protégé to their knees. This army of God's sons is on the verge of being unfolded.

The Lord Jesus was trained and prepared in obscurity. When He was released on the scene, the people were so taken aback that they started asking questions. They could not comprehend what God was doing through Him because of their familiarity with His earthly parents and their circumstances.

We are on the verge of witnessing a repetition of this. A body of people are about to appear who will suddenly explode on the earth, causing men to marvel. These people are being prepared in obscurity by God, but He will manifest them in the open this third day.

Beloved, you are more than you think. God is doing something awesome in your life, and you are on the verge of exploding suddenly upon the earth.

CHAPTER *7*

THE MOUNTAIN OF THE LORD'S HOUSE

In Daniel 2, the Bible records that Nebuchadnezzar, the king of Babylon, had a dream of what would happen at the end of time. In the dream, he saw a big statue that had a head made of gold, a chest made of silver, a trunk of bronze, legs of iron, and feet that were a mixture of iron and clay.

When he rose from his sleep, he tried to recall the dream to no avail, so he summoned all the astrologers and magicians in his kingdom to recall and interpret his dream. His request, however, baffled the astrologers and magicians, who could not fathom how a person could recall another person's dream. They insisted that the king should recall his dream, while they give the interpretation. The king warned that should they fail to recall and interpret his dream, they were doomed, along with their families.

At this time, Daniel was one of the wise men in the kingdom of Babylon. When Daniel heard of the king's decree, he asked to see the king. By the help of the Spirit of God, Daniel was able to recall and interpret the king's dream.

Even after that, Daniel did not walk in this supernatural realm consistently. The Lord allowed him to operate in that realm at the time as a foretaste of the things to come. The third day Christians, on the other hand, will consistently operate in this kind of realm.

Our present church leaders are not the ones who will bring the move of God to completion. Those who will champion the last phase of God's move are presently unknown names. Most of them are currently being raised in obscurity. I am talking about people like you.

You might be unsung and unknown now, but God might be preparing and equipping you to be in the forefront of the last day's move of God on earth, and the Lord is preparing you in obscurity. You might even be ignorant of the fact that the Lord is preparing you for this move. You have prayed and fasted, seeking to be relevant in the now, not knowing that the Lord has been keeping you in obscurity for a purpose.

In the dream that God gave to Nebuchadnezzar, the king saw a statue that had four parts. These four parts symbolized the entire world at that time. The head of gold represented the kingdom of Babylon, which held sway over the entire world in that period. The chest of silver stood for the Medo-Persian kingdom. After Babylon collapsed, Persia had preeminence over the entire world. The trunk of brass represented the kingdom of Greece, the world power that followed when the kingdom of Persia fell. The legs of iron embodied the Roman kingdom, which held sway on the earth until the birth of the Lord Jesus.

After the reign of the legs of iron (the Romans), the feet broke up into ten toes. After the reign of the Romans, no other singular nation would hold sway over the earth. From that moment on, independent nations commenced from Europe. These independent nations represented the iron that could not mix with clay: kingdoms that would be partly strong and partly fragile:

And whereas you saw the feet and toes, partly of potter's clay and partly of iron, the kingdom shall be divided; yet the strength of the iron shall be in it, just as you saw the iron mixed with ceramic clay. And as the toes of the feet were partly of clay, so the kingdom shall be partly strong and partly fragile. As you saw iron mixed with ceramic clay, they will mingle with the seed of men; but they will not adhere to one another, just as iron does not mix with clay. And in the days of these kings the God of heaven will set up a kingdom which shall never be destroyed; and the kingdom shall not be left to other people; it shall break in pieces and consume all these kingdoms, and it shall stand forever. Inasmuch as you saw that the stone was cut out of the mountain without hands, and that it broke in pieces the iron, the bronze, the clay, the silver, and the gold—the great

God has made known to the king what will come to pass after this. The dream is certain, and its interpretation is sure. (Daniel 2:41–45)

Another version [identify version] of the Bible puts verse 45 this way: "And the dream is for the latter times." This dream was also a portrait of the third day church, one which will bring God's move into completion.

These kings represent independent nations that emerged, but God will also set up His kingdom in the days of the kings: "And in the days of these kings the God of heaven will set up a kingdom which shall never be destroyed; and the kingdom shall not be left to other people; it shall break in pieces and consume all these kingdoms, and it shall stand forever" (Daniel 2:44).

In the dream, Nebuchadnezzar saw a mighty rock and an invisible hand that cut a little stone out of the rock. This little stone smote the four kingdoms that had ruled the earth before it and broke them into pieces like the chaff of the summer threshing floors. Then they were blown away, while the stone grew and filled the earth.

The mighty rock represents the Lord Jesus, the invisible hand signifies the Holy Spirit, and the little stone that grew and filled the earth is the church of God: "Then the iron, the clay, the bronze, the silver, and the gold were crushed together, and became like chaff from the summer threshing floors; the wind carried them away so that no trace of them was found. And the stone that struck the image became a great mountain and filled the whole earth" (Daniel 2:35).

When Jesus redeemed man, He redeemed him along with all his inheritance. This implies that the earth was also redeemed when man was. God's original intent when He created the earth was to make it a colony of heaven. He told the nation of Israel that their days would be days of heaven on earth.

When a location is a protectorate of another, it embraces their culture and systems. My country was colonized by Great Britain, so most of the culture and systems embraced in my country belong to the British, including our constitution, which was lifted from the British constitution. The earth was designed to be a colony of heaven. It was meant to embrace the culture and systems of heaven. Unfortunately, this is not presently the position of things on the earth. The devil turned things upside down.

When the Lord created man, He made him the regent of the earth and gave him dominion over the earth. The Hebrew word translated dominion is radar, which means "sovereign rule." Man was given the mandate to rule the earth, and his greatest assignment is the administration of the earth.

The greatest assignment of any pastor is not just to preach, but to administer the lives of people. His preaching should be geared towards the actualization of destiny. He is to administer men towards fulfilling their divine purpose. Whereas the devil has previously engineered people towards fulfilling his evil goals on the earth, the ministers of the gospel, as agents of God, are meant to tailor the lives of men towards fulfilling the program of God for them on the earth.

It is sad to see ministers who merely program their congregations in order to fulfill their own selfish purposes. They tailor them to build their empires, not the kingdom of God. In this third day, many Christian empires are going to crumble and collapse, while others in obscurity will suddenly emerge.

And it shall come to pass in the latter days that the mountain of the Lord's house shall be established on the top of the mountains, and shall be exalted above the hills; and all nations shall flow to it. Many people shall come and say, "Come and let us go up to the mountain of the Lord, to the house of God of Jacob; He will teach us His ways, and we shall walk in His paths." For out of Zion shall go forth the law, and the word of the Lord from Jerusalem. He shall judge between the nations and rebuke many people; they shall beat their swords into plowshares, and their spears into pruning hooks; nation shall not lift up sword against nation, neither shall they learn war anymore. (Isaiah 2:2–4)

CHAPTER 8

THE MOUNTAINS OF SOCIAL IMPACT

There are seven mountains of culture or social impact. As mentioned earlier, the needs of man are in three dimensions: spirit, soul, and body. The avenues through which these three needs are met are in seven categories.

Jerusalem was built on seven hills, the highest being Mount Zion. When David, the restoration king of Israel, was installed as king, he sat on the nation's seat of government in Zion. The church of God is Mount Zion, and she sits on the nations' seats of government.

The seven mountains of culture are part of the domain of the church, and the church is meant to raise the standard on these seven mountains. These are the seven mountains on which human interests are built and nation are built or destroyed :

- Politics
- Commerce
- Education
- Science and technology
- Arts : sports, music, visual arts, entertainment, media etc.
- Religion

- Family

Generally, men carve out kingdoms and empires for themselves from these seven mountains. Those people we regard as celebrities have simply carved a niche for themselves out of one or more of these mountains.

As a result of his rebellion against God, man lost dominion over the earth, and the devil established his kingdom here, thus making him the god of this world even though he is not the legal owner. He usurped man's authority over the earth, and he is the mastermind behind the worldly evil systems controlling most of these seven mountains.

Satan is responsible for the greed, covetousness, selfishness and pride that we see all around, those vices that contravene the plan of God for the earth: "Whose minds the god of this age has blinded, who do not believe, lest the light of the gospel of the glory of Christ, who is the image of God should shine on them" (2 Corinthians 4:4).

God's original plan was that the earth would be a colony of heaven, and that plan has not changed. However, He does not directly engage the devil in battle, since He was not the one who gave the earth to the devil in the first instance. Man did that. God has legally redeemed man from Satan and given him authority to displace the already-defeated devil so that man can recover what he lost.

The devil operates through witchcraft, cults, and mafias to have dominion over the seven mountains of human existence. Witchcraft simply connotes satanic manipulations that seek to control for evil purposes. There are two levels of witchcraft: the principle of witchcraft (based on human manipulations and maneuvers) and the art of witchcraft (the direct involvement of demonic spirits in the manipulation).

In many nations of the earth, the political terrain is dominated by a few people who have constituted the lives into Mafia. In many nations, people's votes do not count during elections. The Mafia manipulates the entire process to suit themselves and their agendas. They decide what happens in the economy of the nation and whether it will improve or decline (except the Lord intervenes).

It is erroneous to assume that the devil should have dominion over the seven mountains of social impact. The church must stop believing that the world belongs to the devil. The earth and its fullness belong to the Lord, not the devil: "The earth is the Lord's and all its fullness, the world and those who dwell therein" (Psalm 24:1).

Some decades ago, believers were well acquainted with a song that says, "Take the whole world and give me Jesus." Based on this wrong attitude, the church watched while the devil reigned in politics, commerce, education, and other mountains of culture in the nations. While a few evil and diabolic people called the Mafia controlled the affairs of the nations of the earth, the church slept, and the enemy took advantage of these mountains. As the devil dominated these seven mountains of social impact, Christians lived in poverty and lost virtually everything. The church was persecuted and suffered until the Lord began to open her eyes to understand the Scriptures.

The twenty-first-century church needs to wake up and stop playing religion. The Lord expects us to go beyond the four walls of our sanctuaries and possess the world. If our impact is restricted to the walls of our meeting places, we are just playing religion—and religion is not of God, but of the devil.

The Lord did not call us to build monasteries, but an army of people who will translate the kingdoms of this world into the kingdom of God and His Christ. The earth is our inheritance, and we must possess it. As joint heirs with the Lord Jesus, we are meant to inherit everything that belongs to Him: "And if children, then heirs of God and joint heirs with Christ, if indeed we suffer with Him, that we may also be glorified together" (Romans 8:17). The earth belongs to the Lord, and He expects the church to possess every territory of the earth, not just a minute portion of it. To achieve this, we must begin to see this truth from God's perspective.

Every Christian has a part to fulfill in God's plan. There is a specific territory allotted for each one of us to occupy. Before a Christian arrives at a certain portion of the earth, a certain ruling spirit will have been operating there. The predominant traits in every region are determined by these ruling spirits. For example, if the spirit of immorality rules in a region, the people living in that location will be immoral.

A missionary who witnessed the gospel and distributed tracts between Argentina and Paraguay shared a testimony of his experience. In Argentina, he was vehemently opposed, but when he crossed over to Paraguay, he gave a tract to a certain woman who accepted it with gratitude. Suddenly he remembered that he had met the same woman earlier in the day in Argentina. She had abused and disdained him in Argentina when he offered her the tract. This shows that there were different spirits operating in the two territories. The spirit operating in Argentina was anti-gospel, while the spirit operating in Paraguay was pro-gospel. This was because the power of the satanic spirit operating initially over Paraguay had been broken and removed in the place of prayer, while the one in Argentina was still intact. The woman exhibited different behavior in the two different territories because she operated under the influence of two contradicting spirits.

People unknowingly pick up the behavior, lifestyle, and culture of the spirits governing the territories where they live. This explains why people in certain nations are more prone to crime and other satanic tendencies than are others. Human beings generally are the same; only our attitudes and cultures differ, based on the spirits operating where we are located. The spirits controlling a territory determine the lifestyle, culture, and behavioral pattern of the people living there.

After the small stone had been carved out of the mighty rock, as described in Nebuchadnezzar's dream, its first assignment was to break into pieces the kingdoms that existed before it. Likewise, for the church of God to establish her dominion over the earth as designed by God, she must overthrow all the former rulers operating within planet earth. If Christians are to take over governments, administrations, and territories in the nations, we must subjugate every other power previously operating in those spheres.

Every Christian must take over the territory he is planted in because God has established him there as a principality. The Lord does not send His people to places He will not go with them. He sends us so that He can win with us, and He expects us to use His authority to unseat the former rulers in those regions.

Whenever a Christian finds himself in a region on the earth, he must study the attitude and culture of the place to discern the kind of spirit or spirits operating there and governing the region. Your dominion as a son of God cannot be established in the place until you subjugate the former ruler(s) in the place of prayer and intercession. If you find yourself excelling in a territory without contending with such former ruler or rulers, it is because other people have paid the price of dethroning them. In most cases, overcoming satanic ruling spirits is not a one-day affair. You must consistently exercise the authority of the Lord to free the region from their influence.

Some believers are not just sent to territories; they are sent to realms. In every nation, there are rulers controlling families, businesses, and the political atmosphere. This explains why the rate of divorce, insolvency, and corruption is higher in some nations than in others. A Christian who has been sent to realms will incapacitate the spirits fighting against such mountains of human existence as marriages, businesses, the political terrain, and the likes.

The nation of Botswana has experienced God's tremendous blessings in terms of economy and good governance, but the enemy attacked their families. The family system in the nation broke down completely. At one point, they recorded the highest rate of HIV/AIDS in the world. People died in the hundreds, including youngsters who committed suicide once they discovered that they were infected with the HIV virus.

To excel as a Christian in such a nation, you must confront and deal with the spirit that attacks the family system. A pastor there once told me that 70 percent of the inhabitants do not know their biological fathers. The family unit within that country can be restored only when the spirit behind that culture is forcefully resisted, overthrown, and ultimately sent off. This is nonnegotiable because the spirit behind their family system is a "pharaoh" who will not let them go easily.

The economy and governance of the nation are doing well because the former rulers governing the territory in those spheres had been dealt with. I once heard of a cabinet minister in Botswana who was summoned because he embezzled four thousand dollars. He responded by committing suicide. There are other nations, however, in which political officeholders take pride in embezzlement. Financial misappropriation is common in those nations because they are subject to the spirit of corruption. To curb economic corruption in such nations, the spirit perpetuating the vice must be dethroned.

When the Lord calls a person to handle problems in the marital, economic, political, or some other sector of human existence, the first thing expected of him is not to print and distribute handbills. He is expected to go into spiritual warfare to curb and dethrone the rulers perpetuating the atrocities. He must deal continually with those spirits that have imposed the problem.

The church of God is called to raise godly standards in the seven mountains of human existence. This implies that the Lord will no longer raise men just to pastor churches.

There are three types of priesthood: the Shemitic, Japhethite, and Hamitic priesthoods. The Shemitic priesthood connotes those who are called into the fivefold ministries. Their major assignment is spiritual. The fivefold ministries help the sons of God to develop their spiritual antennae by teaching them kingdom principles. They are life coaches.

Presently, there is very little spirituality in our churches. Most churches are devoid of visions and revelations, and this is because their congregations are more often subjected to philosophical principles than to kingdom principles. In many instances, satanic orchestrations transpire in many of these churches without the pastor discerning it, which is quite unfortunate.

The Scriptures tell us that Elijah was able to discern what the king of Syria planned in his bedroom. The king of Israel was then able to counter his moves because Elijah discerned the plans. At one point, the Syrian king suspected that there was an agent of Israel in his palace, until one of his subjects told him that there was a prophet in Israel who knew all things by the Spirit of God. Where are the prophets of God today? They are about to be seen, and that includes you and I.

The Japhethite priests are intellectually inclined. These are believers who are trained in life skills such as engineering, sports, commerce, media, and other human endeavors. [changed from "mountains"] Their purpose is to impart knowledge.

The third level of priesthood is the Hamitic priesthood. Some people are of the opinion that Noah cursed Ham, but I do not believe it was a curse, even though Noah had the intent of cursing him.

Noah was a prophet of God, and the supposed curse invoked on Ham was actually a prophecy from God and a blessing in disguise: "Then he said: 'Cursed be Canaan, a servant of servants he shall be unto his brethren'" (Genesis 9:25).

Noah was actually prophesying about Ham's destiny, which was to carry the anointing of servanthood.

For you to understand that this prophecy was not really bad, let us look at this verse of Scripture: "And whosoever desires to be first among you, let him be your slave" (Matthew 20:27). In the kingdom of God, the man who carries the anointing of a servant is the leader. The sons of Ham were made a servant of servants because they were ordained to champion the last move of God!

God reserves the best for last. The nation of Israel, through the sons of Shem, gave the earth spirituality. The sons of Japheth gave intellectuality, while the sons of Ham were ordained to render practical service.

I am not a politician, but I am interested in politics. When God allowed Barack Obama to become the first black president of the United States, it signified that the third day had begun and that there was a shift in the spirit realm. All truths are parallel. Natural things signify what happens in the spirit realm. President Obama is meant to be a servant leader and to serve the nation of America. Unfortunately, there are Christians in that country who criticize him because they do not understand the truth of the Scriptures.

The president of any nation is not empowered by his office, but by the church that understands the plans and programs of God. Only the church has the authority to empower the government of nations, according to the plan of God. In most cases, however, what happens in nations is not always in conformity with the plans and programs of God. When the church fails to influence the government of a nation, the Mafia in that nation will do the influencing and align the nation to the plans of the devil. Any nation thus influenced is bound to experience disaster.

The Hamitic priesthood renders service. They are called to bring practical manifestation to the nations of the earth. God will appoint them as priests on the seven mountains of human existence. He will appoint those who have passed through the Shemitic and Japhethite training. Their intellectual knowledge and skills are based on kingdom principles, and their operations will be based on what they see in the realms of God. They will be planted in banks, schools, conglomerates, and every other human mountain. They will be raised as representatives of God in those places, operating as priests wherever they are planted.

They do not necessarily have to be pastors. In these days that we are in, the titles of men are becoming irrelevant. Divine assignment is not about titles, but about responsibilities. A believer might be a clerical officer in the place of his planting, but he is the person who carries the anointing to execute the programs of God there. God holds him responsible for whatever transpires therein. He must know who he is and understand his mission there. He is there, not just to earn money and pay his bills, but to execute the will of God.

Wherever he finds himself, he is not passive. He is involved in the system, and he is aware of the nitty-gritty and basics of that place. Since he is the one programmed to build the place according to the dictates of God's plan, he is to take responsibility for the place spiritually. For instance, when the place experiences a decline, he ensures that the place is revitalized. As he exercises God's authority and dominion there, the Lord will give him visions and revelations about the true situation of things and also the solution.

He might be a junior staff member there, but his responsibility surpasses that of the chief executive. He gives direction to the place, based on visions and revelations received from God. He is the person ordained by God to give solutions and answers in the place, a reference point to everything transpiring in the place. Even his supposed superiors are answerable to him. He changes the place for God. Those with him in the place rely on what the Spirit of God has to say through him. He gives words of wisdom to the place because he is spiritually inclined.

In the third day, the sons of God will be trained spiritually and dispatched to possess and govern their territories. Millions of Christians will be distributed all over the world.

CHAPTER 9

DISCERNING TERRITORIES

In the preceding chapter, you saw how third day Christians will be appointed to diverse territories on the earth. You were also made to understand that the day of the monastery priesthood is over. However, for you to excel as a third day Christian, you must discern the placement of your territory. Your effectiveness is ensured only when you are located and manifested in the right territory. For example, a believer who is meant to manifest the power of God in the area of marriage will be irrelevant in the area of politics. He will merely cause confusion if he attempts to usurp another person's area of specialty.

Your area of dominion is made manifest in the area of your divine equipment. No one was created to be a jack-of-all-trades. Everyone was created to specialize in a certain divine mission. We were each equipped in an area of specialty from heaven, even before we were formed in our mothers' wombs. No one exists by coincidence on the earth. Every individual was created specifically for divine destiny and a definite mission to attain in the program of God.

No two human beings are the same. Every man has a different inward design that is based on his mission on the earth. For instance, when artisans converge at a building site and open their toolboxes, you can easily discern what they are skilled at doing. Each man's tool defines who he is. An electrician does not carry the tools of a bricklayer. He carries the tools that consolidate his skills or area of specialty.

DISCOVERING YOUR PASSION

What reveals the inward design of a man is his passion. In order to truly discern your mission on earth, you should sit back and identify your passion. This is revealed by what you enjoy doing even when you are not remunerated or compensated.

Your passion is that problem that gets your attention. Once you come in contact with a certain problem in society, you cannot walk away from it. You become focused on providing the desired solution, even when it does not seem to be your business.

For the purpose of effectiveness, you might be expected to create a business, an NGO, or a ministry, or to take a course or get a job along the area of your passion. The main thrust of a believer's service should be along the area of his passion. A person who walks and works in the opposite direction from his passion is wasting his life and destiny.

Every believer who is called into the fivefold ministry must help his congregation or followers to discern, work, and walk in the areas of their passion. Our effectiveness and excellence as individuals become inevitable when we invest all our attention and strength in our passion.

The seven mountains of human existence will be taken over by Christians who invest their time and strength in the area of their passion. This is the kind of army the Lord is unleashing on the world, and if we are to be relevant in the third day church, we must discover the areas of our passion.

Over the years, many ministers have been of the opinion that ministry is about them and not God. While they indulge in lifestyles that contravene their preaching, they go out of their way to convince men with their sugar-coated tongues. There is a shift in the move of God, however. The voices that promulgated the old order will soon sink, while the voices that will liberate the sons of God will soon come into the limelight.

What many ministers are doing presently is to use their congregations to build their empires rather than the kingdom of God. Nevertheless, Jesus Christ said

He would build His church and that the gates of hell would not prevail against it. The Lord cannot fail in His purpose.

Saul's kingdom represented the old order, while the era of David represented the new order. Jonathan was part of the old order, but he was able to identify that a new order was about to unfold, and he wanted to be a part of it. He knew what God was doing, and he identified with it. He even entered into a covenant with the arrowhead of the new order but could not give up his attachment to the old order. Eventually Jonathan perished with the old order because he did not separate himself from it.

When the order of the third day church emerges, the former order will fizzle out. Those who refuse to separate themselves from the former order will be set aside with it. The end-time world will be ruled by the third day church. She will operate from heaven and function in Christ on the earth.

EPILOGUE

Beloved, we are living in the last days. We are living in the day of God's manifestation of awesome power and glory, and we are privileged to be a part of what the Lord will be doing on the face of the earth in this season.

God does not want you to be like Jonathan, who had a revelation of the Davidic era but could not separate from the old, rejected order of Saul. He perished with that old order of Saul. He does not want you to be like Samson, who was subdued on the lap of a strange woman. He does not want you to act like the portion of Gideon's army that lapped the water with their mouths.

The hour has come when the exceeding power of God will incapacitate all the atrocities of the devil on the earth. God will not use trees or stones to achieve these feats; He wants to use you and every other person who is willing to operate from His presence.

The days of operating from the monasteries of men are over. This is a new dawn. Press into His presence.